CONTENTS

GENERAL LEARNING OBJECTIVES OF THIS UNIT

This Open Learning Unit will supply you with all the core information you need to answer an examination question or to write an essay on attention and skills learning. It will take you three to four hours to work through, though if you attempt all the suggested activities, it might well take longer.

By the end of this Unit you should:

▷ be familiar with three alternative models of selective attention and the capacity model of attention, and understand their limitations;

▷ understand the distinction between automatic and attentional processing;

▷ be aware of factors affecting sustained attention.

1 Selective Attention

KEY AIMS: By the end of Part 1 you will be able to:

▷ *Define attention*
▷ *Explain why psychologists study attention*
▷ *Describe Broadbent's model of selective attention and its limitations*
▷ *Describe two other bottleneck models of selective attention and show how they overcome the limitations of Broadbent's model.*

Paying attention*?

It used to be a popular joke that the former US President Ronald Reagan couldn't walk and chew gum at the same time. Can you? Almost certainly you can because these activities are typically automatic — we can do them without paying attention. We can walk, chew gum and pay attention to music or plan an essay or daydream about a holiday. Quite a lot of everyday skills don't need our full attention — though they may have done at first. For example, a toddler will put a tremendous amount of concentration and mental effort into trying to feed itself and its first few months of walking.

What other activities can you think of that needed your full attention to start with but now need less?

An example for me would be learning to swim. It took me months to co-ordinate my arms, legs and breathing to do the Australian crawl. If my attention wandered I would breathe in at the wrong moment and swallow a mouthful of chlorinated water. Another example is driving. At first everything requires attention and mental effort; steering and changing gear at the same time is impossibly difficult. Later you are able to drive safely and listen to a play on the radio or talk to your passengers at the same time.

These examples show us that we can *divide* our attention. For some tasks though we need to *focus* our attention or *selectively attend** to a particular sensory input. In fact there is an astonishing range of sensory inputs reaching us all the time.

SOMETHING TO TRY

Note down how many sounds there are going on around you now — sounds from the street, conversations, TV, radio, music, insects, rustling leaves? There are probably many different sounds you could focus on but have been ignoring.

Now write down all the other sensations you are aware of — attend not only to your senses but also your memories, thoughts and daydreams.

Now focus on a particular stimulus — ideally listen to some music. See if you can listen to just a single part of it; the bass line, or the piano part, or a singer's voice. You will see that we can focus down on a very specific stimulus from a very wide range; we can selectively attend.

Why study attention?

In the very early days of psychology, attention was an important topic and pioneers like William James (1890) devoted a lot of time to it. However, early researchers mostly used a subjective and not very scientific method called introspection* to investigate it. Introspection involves training observers to report on their own conscious experience. Unfortunately, different observers may report similar experiences differently and vice versa. As our private experience is not open to public inspection the truth cannot be established objectively. Although scientists attempted to be as objective as possible, this serious difficulty soon led to the abandonment of introspection as a technique.

In the early years of the twentieth century a young American psychologist, John Watson, sought to make psychology a more objective and scientific discipline by limiting research to topics that could be objectively observed and measured. Behaviour could be observed and measured; the inner workings of the mind could not. Watson's new science of behaviourism* quickly came to dominate psychology and by 1920 the study of behaviour was 'in' and the study of mind (including attention) was definitely 'out'.

So far I have not clearly defined attention. It is quite difficult to pin down. William James (1890) wrote 'everyone knows what attention is' and went on to define it as selecting one stimulus for conscious attention from several. Govier and Govier (1991) claim that 'The study of attention is really the study of consciousness'. They suggest that the term 'attention' became popular because 'consciousness' raised so many hackles among behaviourists and is itself so difficult to define. Now it is generally used to refer to both selective attention and to the automatic processes which for example allow an adult to walk without the conscious attention a toddler needs.

The study of mind gradually returned to psychology in the 1950s and attention was one of the topics that led the way. A number of factors brought the study of mind back into psychology:

(i) Practical problems in helping people to use new electronic technology and control systems: for example, how to maximize the signal detection rate with radar and sonar screens; how to select out which messages to attend to in air-traffic control by ground-to-air radio.

(ii) New machines such as electronic computers offered a new information-processing approach to understanding the inner workings of the mind.

(iii) The development of operational definitions of internal mental processes made research into how we process information acceptable within a scientific framework.

(iv) A new machine, the audio tape recorder, made new sorts of research possible.

The study of cognition in general, and attention in particular, has become progressively more relevant as control systems become more ever-present and more complex. We probably all accept for example that road accidents are more often the result of operator error (when drivers make mistakes) than engineering failure. Reason's (1987) very readable psychologist's account of the Chernobyl accident highlights the role of such human factors in the events leading up to the nuclear plant going out of control.

The cocktail party phenomenon. The communications revolution led psychologists to think of the mind as an information-processing machine, like a computer or a telephone exchange. One of the first psychologists to think in this way was Colin Cherry (1953) who identified the 'cocktail party' phenomenon. Imagine you are at a party with a couple of friends — any party will do, you don't have to be drinking a cocktail. It is highly likely that you will be paying attention to your own conversation and ignoring half a dozen others; in fact you will have no idea what others around you are saying. Now, imagine that someone in a conversation you are not paying attention to mentions your name. There is a very good chance that you would hear it.

A POSSIBLE PROJECT

The cocktail party phenomenon is something I will refer to throughout this Unit. Can you think of a way to test Cherry's observation scientifically? Could this be a suitable project? Read the rest of the Unit before you finalize your design — you will find a lot more ideas.

So far, I have raised a number of issues about attention.

1. How can we explain our ability to selectively attend to one stimulus without being continually distracted by many others?
2. Are non-attended stimuli ignored completely and, if so, how can we explain the cocktail party phenomenon?
3. What can we do automatically and what can we do only if we pay attention?
4. How many things can we pay attention to at any one time?

Bottleneck models of attention

A bottleneck restricts the rate of flow. The narrower the bottleneck, the lower the rate of flow. Roadworks on a motorway can have a bottleneck effect by restricting traffic flow. The three models of attention which follow start from the observation that we cannot consciously attend to all of our sensory input at once. This limited capacity for paying attention is therefore a bottleneck and all three models try to explain how the material that passes through the bottleneck is selected.

FIGURE 1. *Air-traffic controllers at work.*

Broadbent's filter model*

Donald Broadbent (1958) looked at air-traffic control type problems in a laboratory. He wanted to see how people were able to focus their attention (selectively attend), and to do this he deliberately overloaded them with stimuli — they had too many signals, too much information, to process at the same time. One of the ways Broadbent achieved this was by simultaneously sending one message (a 3-digit number) to a person's right ear and a different message (a different 3-digit number) to their left ear. Participants were asked to listen to both messages at the same time and repeat what they heard. This is known as a dichotic listening* task.

In the example below the participant hears three digits in their right ear (8,3,7) and three digits in their left ear (2,9,1). Broadbent was interested in how these would be repeated back. Would the participant repeat the digits back in the order that they were heard and repeat what was heard in one ear followed by the other ear?

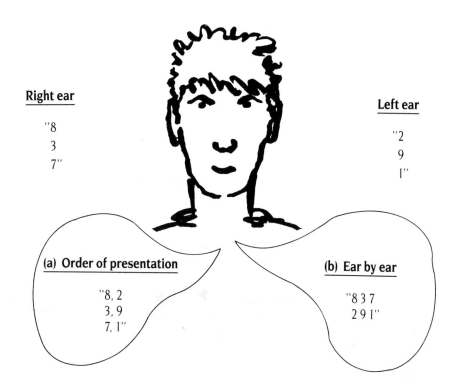

Right ear

"8
3
7"

Left ear

"2
9
1"

(a) Order of presentation

"8, 2
3, 9
7, 1"

(b) Ear by ear

"8 3 7
2 9 1"

FIGURE 2. *A dichotic listening task.*

Broadbent found that people made fewer mistakes repeating back ear by ear and would usually repeat back in this way.

 SOMETHING TO TRY

Broadbent's research using the dichotic listening method is something you could try using a couple of personal cassette players with an earpiece from each one attached to a different ear. Which method of repeating back do your participants use if not instructed? Which method produces the fewest errors?

Single channel model. Results from this research led Broadbent to produce his 'filter' model of how selective attention works. Broadbent concluded that we can pay attention to only one channel at a time — so his is a *single channel* model. But what does he mean by a channel?

In the dichotic listening task experiment each ear is a channel*. We can listen either to the right ear (that's one channel) or the left ear (that's another channel). Broadbent also discovered that it is difficult to switch channels more than twice a second. So, you can only pay attention to the message in one ear at a time —

the message in the other ear is lost, though you may be able to repeat back a few items from the unattended ear. This could be explained by the short-term memory store* which holds on to information in the unattended ear for a short time (see the companion Unit, *Remembering and Forgetting* for more information on the short-term memory store).

The most important point is that Broadbent thought that the filter, which selects one channel for attention, does this *only* on the basis of the *physical characteristics* of the information coming in: for example, which particular ear the information was coming to, or the type of voice. According to Broadbent, the *meaning* of any of the messages is not taken into account at all by the filter. All *semantic processing** (processing the information to decode the meaning, in other words understanding what is said) is carried out after the filter has selected the channel to pay attention to. So, whatever message is sent to the unattended ear is not understood.

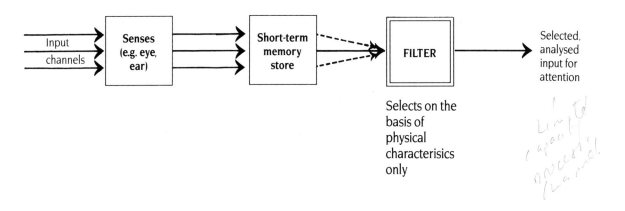

FIGURE 3. *Broadbent's filter model.*

SAQ 1

Using Broadbent's model, which of these channels could the filter tell apart?

Left ear: (i) *woman reading novel*   *Right ear:* (i) *man reading novel*

(ii) *woman reading crossword*   (ii) *woman reading novel backwards*

(iii) *man giving exam instructions*   (iii) *man reading nursery rhymes*

Is Broadbent right? Think back to Cherry's cocktail party phenomenon. Does Broadbent's model predict or allow for this? As you may have worked out, Broadbent's model predicts that hearing your name when you are not paying attention should be impossible because unattended messages are filtered out before you process the sound to extract the meaning. There is, therefore, no way in which you should be able to hear anything — either your name, or a comment such as 'darling, your trousers have caught fire' — if you are not already paying attention to that particular voice.

Other researchers demonstrated the cocktail party effect under experimental conditions and began to identify the circumstances in which information heard in the unattended ear 'broke through' to interfere with what you were paying attention to in the other ear. For example, two students, Gray and Wedderburn (1960) used a dichotic listening task similar to Broadbent's in figure 2 and found that students could put material from both ears together so that it made sense.

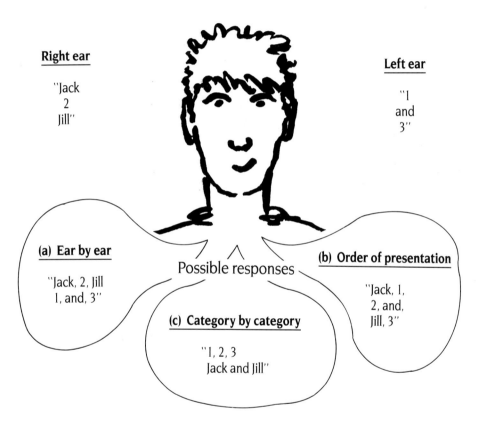

Right ear

"Jack
2
Jill"

Left ear

"1
and
3"

(a) Ear by ear

"Jack, 2, Jill
1, and, 3"

Possible responses

(b) Order of presentation

"Jack, 1,
2, and,
Jill, 3"

(c) Category by category

"1, 2, 3
Jack and Jill"

Gray and Wedderburn found that participants were able to give a category by category response (i.e. one which made sense of the material they heard, as shown in (c) above), which Broadbent's filter model predicts would not be possible.

FIGURE 4. *Gray and Wedderburn's dichotic listening task.*

Speech shadowing. Much more research, though, was carried out by Anne Treisman using the speech shadowing* method. In this, participants were asked to simultaneously repeat aloud speech played in one ear (called the 'attended' ear) whilst another message was spoken to the other ear (see figure 5).

Treisman carried out a number of experiments like this. For example, she found that if she played a passage in English to the attended ear for shadowing and the same passage in French to the other ear, most of her bilingual participants would notice that both had the same meaning. In another experiment, a passage was read to one ear and lists of words to the other ear. Part way through, the messages swapped ears. The 'shadowers' followed the swap and continued to shadow the narrative passage — in fact some didn't realize that they had switched ears.

Attended ear

"So Jane Eyre picked up her needlework and thought how nice it would be to go to a disco ..."

Unattended ear

"12 down, 'Every cocktail should have one on a stick.' 6 letters. First letter c."

So Jane Eyre picked up her needlework and thought how nice it would be to go to a disco ...

Treisman asked participants to 'shadow' a passage presented in one ear (the attended ear) by repeating it aloud as they heard it.

FIGURE 5. *Speech shadowing.*

Attended ear

"Jane watched the new video strange comet had tumber world said smile table ..."

Unattended ear

"Dissect purple enough it when rose avocado train she did not think that her mother would like it at all ..."

Jane watched the new video, she did not think that her mother would like it at all ...

Treisman found that participants could switch ears to follow a prose passage being shadowed.

FIGURE 6. *Switching ears in speech shadowing.*

Put together, the evidence suggests that Broadbent's filter model is not adequate. It does not allow for meaning being taken into account before filtering takes place.

Briefly outline Broadbent's Filter model. Give three reasons (or pieces of evidence) which suggest that it does not fully explain selective attention.

Treisman's attenuation model*

Treisman modified Broadbent's model to overcome these difficulties. Selective attention requires that stimuli are filtered so that attention is directed. Broadbent's model suggests that the selection of material to attend to (that is, the filtering) is made early, before semantic analysis. Treisman's model retains this early filter which works on physical features of the message only. The crucial difference is that Treisman's filter *attenuates* rather than eliminates the unattended material. Attenuation is like turning down the volume so that if you have four sources of sound in one room (TV, radio, people talking, baby crying) you can turn down or attenuate three in order to attend to the fourth. The result is almost the same as turning them off; the unattended material appears lost. But if a nonattended channel includes your name, there is a chance that you will hear it — because although the material has been attenuated it is still there.

Treisman also adds a second filter which analyses further the stimuli entering the attended (unattenuated) channel as well as some of the attenuated material, if it is relevant.

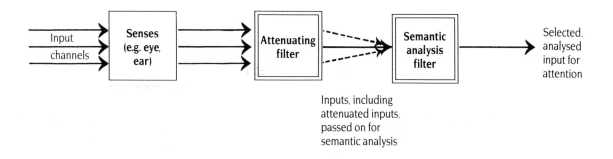

FIGURE 7. *Treisman's attenuation model.*

To be analysed, items have to reach a certain threshold* level of intensity. All the attended/selected material will reach this threshold but only some of the attenuated items. Some items will have a permanently reduced threshold, for example your own name or words and phrases like 'help', 'fire' and 'watch out'. Other items will have a reduced threshold at a particular moment if they have some relevance to the main attended message.

Treisman's model overcomes some of the problems with Broadbent's but it still leaves us with unanswered questions. It does not explain how exactly semantic analysis works; the idea of attenuation is not explained and it may be that the first filter (which works on the physical features of the message) is not needed at all, because its work is done by the second filter.

SAQ
3

(a) Outline how Treisman's model is different to Broadbent's.

(b) If you were talking about classical music to a friend and someone else said the name 'Mozart', would you be more likely to hear it than if they had said the name 'Smith'? Give your reasons.

(c) What words might have a reduced threshold for you but not for another person?

(d) How does Treisman's model explain the cocktail party phenomenon?

Deutsch and Deutsch's late selection model*

Deutsch and Deutsch solve the problems posed by the Broadbent model in a different way to Treisman. Their model suggests that all inputs* are subject to high level semantic analysis before a filter selects material for conscious attention. Selection is therefore late because it occurs after items have been recognized rather than before as in Broadbent's model. Selection is 'top-down'* in that an item which has relevance to you — your name for example — or is in context, is likely to be selected. Material is identified or recognized, it's relevance, value and importance weighed and the most relevant is passed upwards for conscious attention.

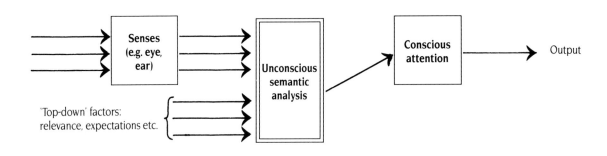

FIGURE 8. *Deutsch and Deutsch's late selection model.*

Some support for a late selection model is offered by research which shows that an unattended message in a dichotic listening task can affect behaviour even though the listener has no conscious awareness of hearing the unattended message. For example, Moray (1969) paired an electric shock with a word over several trials so that the person became conditioned to produce a detectable change in galvanic skin response (GSR — electrical resistance of the skin) when the word was spoken. He found that several of his participants produced a change in GSR when the word occurred in an unattended message even though they were not aware of hearing it.

Another interesting piece of research is by McKay (1973). Using ambiguous words like 'bark' he instructed participants to shadow an ambiguous sentence while, in the unattended ear, a word was played which could clarify the meaning of the sentence. Later, participants who were quite unaware at a conscious level of the word in their unattended ear, chose meanings for the ambiguous sentence they had shadowed which were in line with the unattended word.

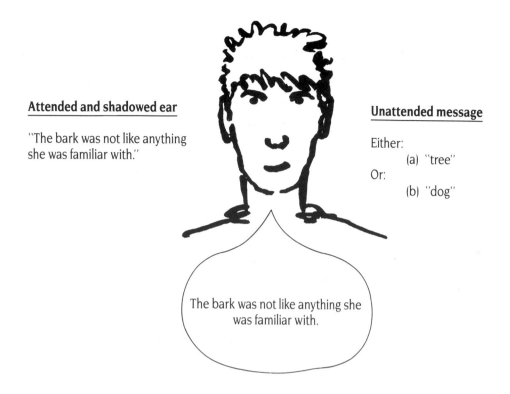

Attended and shadowed ear

"The bark was not like anything she was familiar with."

Unattended message

Either:

    (a) "tree"

Or:

    (b) "dog"

The bark was not like anything she was familiar with.

The word in the unattended ear will affect the participant's interpretation of the shadowed message in the attended ear.

FIGURE 9. *Shadowing ambiguous sentences.*

For example, participants who shadowed the sentence in figure 8 above and who heard the word 'tree' in their unattended ear were more likely to pick sentence 1 below and those who heard the word 'dog' in their unattended ear were more likely to pick sentence 2.

    Sentence 1 — *'She had not seen wood like this before.'*

    Sentence 2 — *'The animal made a very strange noise.'*

Later research has to some extent supported the work of Moray and McKay. For example, Corteen and Wood (1972) found results similar to Moray's using better equipment.

However, Newstead and Dennis (1979) found that a word such as 'tree' or 'dog' only had the effect claimed for it when it came from an otherwise silent, unattended channel. Similarly, Dawson and Schell (1982) could only find reliable changes in GSR when the conditioned word was fed to the left ear. (This has implications for our understanding of which hemisphere of the brain processes emotionally important stimuli.) Research continues to show that under some circumstances unattended material may receive some degree of analysis. Wexler (1988), for example, found that a GSR response varied not only according to the ear of presentation but also according to the personality of the listener.

Studies such as these can be seen as supporting the late selection model. However, it is a little implausible that *all* material is analysed for meaning — it would take up a lot of processing capacity and this would not be very economical as much of the material would not reach conscious attention at all. Treisman's model could also account for the data we have mentioned — a word in the unattended ear could have a reduced threshold because of its relevance, so perhaps on the grounds of economy we should prefer Treisman's model.

SOMETHING TO TRY

Look back at how McKay's study of ambiguous sentences was carried out. Can you carry out similar research? You may be able to develop this into a full-scale project.

You will need two personal cassette players with headphones, and you will need to create some more ambiguous sentences and words. Participants could, for example, be played and asked to shadow, an ambiguous sentence in their attended ear while at the same time a disambiguating word is played in their unattended ear. They are then given a list of sentences and are asked to select the sentence closest in meaning to the sentence they shadowed. Will their choice reflect the disambiguating word? For example, if the ambiguous sentence is 'Helen started the engine and pulled away from the bank' and the disambiguating word is 'money', will participants select a sentence which reflects the identification of bank with money rather than river?

Explain how the findings of Moray and McKay can or cannot be explained by:

(a) *The Deutsch and Deutsch model;*

(b) *The Treisman model;*

(c) *The Broadbent model.*

Hint — *You will need to know exactly how material is selected for conscious attention in each of the three models — in other words, how unattended material is filtered out.*

Checklist

1. Attention, from an information processing standpoint, is examined through purely hypothetical information flow models. Such models have no basis in neuroanatomy.

2. Nevertheless these cognitive models were created as tools through which to attempt to explain and predict observed behaviour and ultimately to solve real human problems.

3. Broadbent's model is a milestone, but later research suggests it cannot account for all the phenomena of selective attention.

4. Subsequent models can account for all the phenomena but only at the expense of undesirable complexity.

Automatic and Attentional Processing

KEY AIMS: By the end of Part 2 you will be able to:

▷ *Distinguish between serial and parallel processing*
▷ *Explain under what circumstances parallel processing is possible*
▷ *Describe Kahnemann's capacity model of attention and how capacity is allocated.*

Dividing attention

So far, we have looked at how we can explain how we selectively attend to some stimuli and ignore others. However, there are, as I mentioned earlier, many situations in which attention seems to be divided, for which a model of selective attention may not be useful. For example, driving and chatting or driving and listening to the radio are examples of doing more than one thing at the same time. An important element here is that these tasks use different sensory modes* for input. Driving draws mainly on visual input whereas chatting and listening are auditory skills.

Allport *et al.* (1972) demonstrated this experimentally by asking people to do two tasks at once. For example, they showed that people were able to shadow and memorize speech while also memorizing some complicated pictures — in fact they performed as well on both tasks together as when the tasks were done singly.

15

Schaffer (1975) devised similar tasks using skilled audiotypists. He found that his participants could type material presented visually, even if it was in an unfamiliar language, while simultaneously shadowing speech heard through headphones. However, he found that performance was badly affected if the two tasks interfered with each other in terms of either input or output (for example, if the passage to be shadowed had to be read as well as the passage to be typed, or if both passages were heard through headphones, one to each ear, one to be typed and the other to be shadowed).

 SOMETHING TO TRY

Think of a skill that you possess — knitting, driving, riding a horse, riding a bicycle, writing, etc. — and try to establish what other kinds of things you can do together with your skill without interference, and what causes a drop in performance. Does this support the idea that using different input/output modes causes less interference?

Interference caused by tasks using the same input and output modes is not a complete explanation though. Have you noticed how a driver may temporarily drop out of a conversation when a difficult driving situation arises — a difficult road junction or an unexpected manoeuvre by another driver? The two tasks — driving and chatting — don't interfere with each other most of the time but they seem to do so when the driving gets more difficult. Perhaps the answer lies in the extent to which tasks can be done automatically.

 SOMETHING TO TRY

Few of us are skilled audiotypists but we may have other skills that we could use to investigate interference as Allport et al. did. If you are a member of a group of students with access to a computer video game, could you devise a full-scale project along the lines of Allport's research? For example, will a skilled video game player produce a lower score if asked to shadow a passage presented over headphones at the same time as playing a video game?

Attention and skill

William James introduced the idea of automatic performance* — doing a task which does not require conscious, focused attention. As we saw earlier, we all possess quite a number of skills that we can do which may have required a great deal of attention at first but are now automatic. Clearly our everyday lives would be much more restricted if we had to concentrate for walking, getting dressed, tying shoelaces and all the other skilled behaviours we have learnt to do automatically, in the way that a learner driver has to during a first lesson. Once a skill is acquired though, it can be trotted out automatically, without a thought.

Shiffrin and Schneider (1977) carried out a series of studies to investigate automatic skilled performance in more depth. They concluded that two distinct modes of information processing could be identified.

1. Serial processing*. Stimuli are processed in series, one at a time. Attention is focused on one stimulus; listening to one ear in a dichotic listening task, for example. This mode of processing is flexible, attention can be directed to any stimulus, but is of limited capacity. We cannot attend to both messages in a dichotic listening task. This is the mode of processing that the selective attention models of Broadbent, Treisman and Deutsch and Deutsch refer to.

2. Parallel processing*. This is an automatic form of information processing. Several tasks can be performed at the same time in parallel, for example driving and talking. It takes a lot of practice for a task to become automatic (you cannot learn to swim or type overnight). Once learned, automatic processing is hard to modify but it can be done without conscious attention and without an obvious capacity limit.

SOMETHING TO TRY

Handwriting is also largely automatic. We don't have to concentrate as hard as we did when we first tried to do joined-up writing.

Try following one of the star shapes printed below, keeping a pencil line in between the two parallel lines and you will see how hard it is to modify an automatic skill. Place a mirror immediately in front of the star shape so that you can see it reflected. Now try to draw around the star, keeping within the parallel lines, while looking in the mirror, not directly at the sheet of paper.

 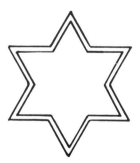

Support for this distinction between serial and parallel processing is also drawn from research into visual search carried out by Treisman and Gelade (1980). They asked people to search for a target item embedded in a visual display.

In the first condition participants were asked to detect a target item on the basis of one of two possible features, for example either any letter coloured grey (one feature), or a letter 'S' (the other feature). The target was embedded in a background of up to 30 distracting items of, for example, white letter 'T's or black letter 'X's. See if you can find the target item in figure 10.

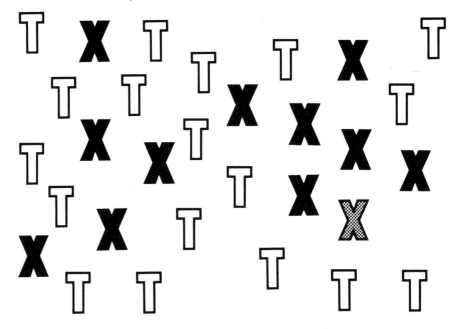

FIGURE 10.

In the second condition participants were asked to search for a target item in which two features occurred together, for example a black (one feature) letter 'T' (the other feature). See if you can find the target item in figure 11.

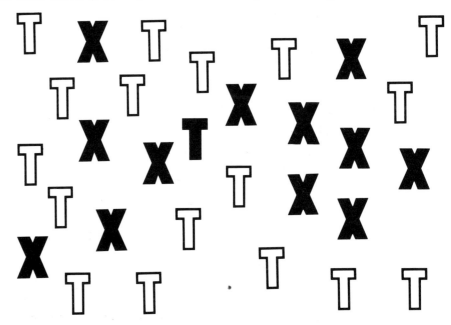

FIGURE 11.

Did it take you longer to find the target item in figure 11 than in figure 10? Treisman and Gelade showed their participants lots of displays like the ones you have looked at, except that they used coloured letters rather than the black, white and grey we are restricted to. Not all the displays had a target and they gradually increased their size from one item to five, then fifteen and finally thirty items. They found that as they increased the size of the displays, participants took more and more time to find the target in the second condition but not in the first. Both conditions require participants to search for two features, either a grey letter or a letter 'S' in the first condition, or two features combined — a black 'T' — in the second condition; so why the difference in performance?

In the first condition participants seem to be able to scan the display very quickly for either of the two possible features. This seems to be done in parallel, automatically. In the second condition participants have to be sure that both features are present in the same item, in effect an *object* has to be identified rather than a *feature*. Attention has to be focused to scan each item one at a time, in series. Therefore as the size of the visual display increases, the difference in time taken between conditions one and two increases. In condition one, you can find a grey letter or a letter 'S' almost as quickly in a display of thirty items as in one of five items. But in condition two serial processing means that each additional item in the display is another item to be processed.

A POSSIBLE PROJECT

A visual search study of the sort carried out by Treisman and Gelade could be the basis of a full-scale project. If you designed a series of visual displays with varying numbers of items in them for each of the two conditions, would your findings support those of Treisman and Gelade? You may need assistance from your tutor in designing this study so as to control all variables and it may be helpful to see the original article. You will find the reference at the end of the Unit.

In practice most tasks require a mixture of both serial and parallel processing. In driving a car, focused attention may be required for making some decisions, but not for gear changing. You will also find that there is a limit to overall capacity — try speech shadowing, knitting, memorizing 38 objects placed on a table and dancing a waltz simultaneously, and I think you will agree.

SAQ
5

(a) *What is serial processing?*

(b) *What is parallel processing?*

(c) *Briefly explain how it is possible to do more than one task at once. Use examples from your own experience.*

Capacity model*

Kahneman (1973) has proposed a model of attention which takes account of the combination of automatic performance, and performance requiring focused attention. He abandons the single channel serial processing ideas of Broadbent, Treisman and Deutsch and Deutsch; instead he proposes a 'central processor'* which has an ability to allocate attention. So, you can converse while driving but the driving has first call on focused attention and if all of it is needed at a sticky moment then you will stop talking until spare capacity is available again. Capacity will vary with your level of arousal and within overall limits.

One way to think of available capacity is as a pipe of flexible diameter. If you are tired and/or underaroused you will have less processing capacity than when you are at a peak of wide-awake alertness.

Not all available capacity is needed at any one time. You might daydream when knitting or cycling along a quiet lane because these activities are largely automatic and require little attention, even though they may be complex and have required a lot of conscious attention once. The idea of 'mental effort' can be used to express how much conscious attention is needed. Writing an essay in an exam takes most of your attention and a lot of mental effort.

So far, Kahneman's model seems very useful in that it explains how we combine focused attention and automatic processing. Can it explain some of the problems we considered earlier, for example the cocktail party phenomenon? To answer this we need to look at what Kahneman says about how the central processor allocates attention.

How attention is allocated. According to Kahneman, two sorts of factor are involved in the allocation of attention.

(a) Moment-by-moment intentions. You allocate attention to what you are concentrating on: learning to drive a car, planning an essay, etc.

(b) Factors which 'grab' your attention because they are important to you. (Kahneman calls these enduring dispositions*.)

We may find our attention grabbed by things in a quite personal or idiosyncratic way. For example, I used to drive a 1950s Morris Minor car and I still notice other Morris Minors when I'm driving. Someone else might notice clothes, or birds, and an architect might notice things about a house that you or I miss. However, there are other 'enduring dispositions' that we will have in common, such as someone saying 'look out, behind you' or a fire bell or the smell of food cooking if we are hungry.

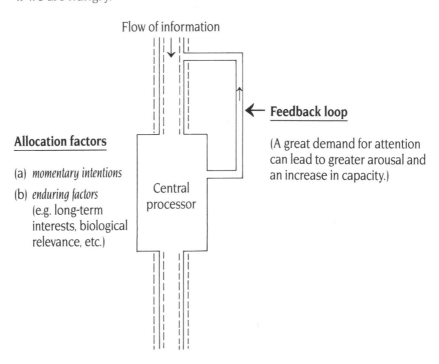

FIGURE 12. *Factors affecting allocation of attention in central processor.*

SOMETHING TO TRY

What has grabbed your attention today? Make a short list.

Biologically important stimuli. The pattern which emerges is that things which have some biological relevance — in other words, importance for our health, welfare and survival, will gain our attention.

Physically arresting or novel stimuli. As well as being 'grabbed' by stimuli that are important, we are also likely to be grabbed by stimuli that are vivid or intense, (a loud noise, a strong smell, an arresting image), or are new and novel. For example, a domestic cat is not a very intense stimulus but if one appeared in a psychology class its novelty would probably ensure that it distracted everyone.

Can Kahneman's model explain the cocktail party phenomenon? How?

*(**Hint** — you can compare capacity allocated in Kahneman's model with the filtering mechanisms in the three filter models.)*

Do you prefer Kahneman's explanation to the three filter models considered earlier? Give your reasons.

Kahneman's capacity model can certainly account for the material we have considered so far. If we assume that there is some central capacity which can be allocated flexibly, then more than one item can be processed simultaneously so long as the demands made do not exceed the overall capacity limit. However, the capacity model has been criticized for failing to give more than a superficial explanation. For example, if task A can be undertaken in parallel with task B, then we might assume that one of the tasks is being processed automatically. On the other hand, if task A interferes with task B, then we might take this as evidence for a capacity limit. Allport (1980) suggests that such reasoning 'merely soothes away curiosity by the appearance of providing an explanation'.

Eysenck and Keane (1990) suggest that a further problem occurs when we look at the interactions of four tasks. If task A interferes with task C more than task B does, then it seems reasonable to conclude that task A uses more processing capacity than task B. What happens, though, if we find the opposite happens when we look at interference with a further task, task D? If task B interferes with task D more than task A does, what conclusions can we now reach? We cannot account for this sort of finding — and Eysenck and Keane quote such research — with a simple capacity model.

A possible solution can be found by turning to the developing work of cognitive neuropsychologists — scientists who approach cognition from the direction of neuroscience rather than information processing, in essence, using knowledge of the cognitive performance of people with brain damage to build up a picture of cognitive processes in general. Cognitive neuropsychologists take a modular* approach — that is they assume that processing is carried out by fairly independent, anatomically distinct *processors* or *modules* — an approach associated with Fodor. A modular approach can solve the four-task problem by getting us to look at the similarities of two tasks rather than at an overall capacity limit. Thus task A may interfere with task C not because too much processing capacity is needed, but because the two tasks are similar, use the same modules, and interfere with each other.

21

There are clearly major differences between the 'wet' neuropsychology approach and the 'dry' information processing approach. A capacity model can explain how task difficulty can affect two-task performance, whereas a modular model can explain how task similarity can affect two-task performance. It is therefore not surprising that attempts have been made to combine them into a hierarchy of processes with a coordinating central processor above and a number of modules below. Norman and Shallice (1980), for example, propose a three-stage model and Logan (1988) goes further in seeking to explain how memory is involved in the development of automatic processing. These models are interesting and reward further study, but are beyond our scope here.

Checklist

1. Serial processing refers to focusing attention on one stimulus at a time.

2. Parallel processing refers to an ability to perform more than one task at the same time if one of the tasks can be performed automatically and without focused attention.

3. Many tasks combine both serial and parallel processing.

4. Kahnemann's capacity model can account for both automatic and attentional processes but has been criticized as superficial.

Sustained Attention

KEY AIMS: By the end of Part 3 you will be able to:

▷ *List five factors which make vigilance tasks difficult*
▷ *Show how arousal and performance are thought to be related*
▷ *Explain how performance on a vigilance task may be improved.*

Sustained attention or vigilance

Like selective attention, work on sustained attention* or vigilance* began in the 1940s with military problems arising from the Second World War. For example, Mackworth (1950) devised a laboratory task which simulated the problems of detecting submarines from patrolling aircraft. Each participant watched a clock-like device on which a pointer moved one step every second. Twelve times every 30 minutes, at random, the pointer would jump two steps instead of one. The person had to detect this and press a key.

Vigilance tasks are usually of quite a long duration (Mackworth's task lasted two hours), target signals may be infrequent or absent altogether, and they may be very brief and hard to detect. The vigilance task is externally paced (the operator's rate of work is outside his or her control and it is not possible to take a break) and it is monotonous.

Mackworth's experiment was successful in replicating the sort of military experience, such as watching a radar or sonar screen, which the government was interested in. He found that participants' performance was 85% correct in the first 30 minutes, 74% correct in the next 30 minutes and 70% correct after this.

 Do you think this research has other non-military uses? Can you think of other tasks which require vigilance?

In fact, there are many monitoring, inspection and quality control tasks which are quite like the one Mackworth devised; for example, flying an aircraft for a long time on a steady course, monitoring a power station, proofreading, examining metal components, checking finished pottery, and acting as anaesthetist during an operation.

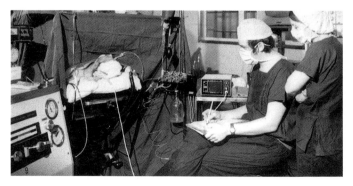

FIGURE 13. *An anaesthetist at work.*

▶ How can performance on vigilance tasks be improved and the fall-off in performance, demonstrated by Mackworth, which happens in the first 30 minutes or so, be prevented?

Improving vigilance performance

Often, in the workplace, there is no check on the accuracy of the operator's vigilance: signals may go undetected (a false negative*), nonexistent signals may be reported (a false positive*), and the operator has no way of knowing how well he or she is doing.

One very successful idea is to give feedback or knowledge of results. If a person is told immediately whenever they fail to spot a signal or raise a false alarm their performance improves dramatically. Why? First, this gives the person information about sequences of events so that they are better able to predict and be ready for signals. Having some idea of what to expect is a big help, though if circumstances change — inspecting a different product for example — it may take a while for new expectations to form and accuracy will be reduced temporarily. Second, knowledge of results helps to motivate people.

(?) *Does your experience of academic work support this? If you have prompt knowledge of results, does this affect how hard you work? Do you feel more motivated?*

Another way of improving performance is to raise the person's level of arousal. Vigilance tasks are generally very boring and the decline in performance found by Mackworth in the first hour or so of a task may be due to a decline in arousal. This is supported by other research which shows changes in heart rate, galvanic skin response and EEG* associated with lower levels of arousal.

SOMETHING TO TRY

Can you place each of these three drivers on the arousal and performance curve in figure 14?

Driver A *is coming back from a wedding reception at 3.00 a.m. He has been awake for 21 hours, he has been driving down an empty motorway for two hours, the car is very warm and the passengers are all asleep.*

Driver B *is stuck in a traffic jam on the motorway. She has four children and a dog in a small car and is an hour late for her check-in time at the airport. Two children are fidgeting and another has just been sick over the dog. She has a growing headache and the radio is playing very loud.*

Driver C *is calmly thinking about a meeting in 30 minutes' time. She is on time, relaxed and wide awake. The car is smooth and quiet, the road is wide and curves gently through the edge of scenic parkland.*

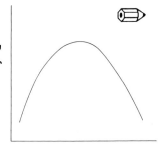

FIGURE 14. *The relationship between arousal and performance is often thought of as an inverted U curve. Performance is good at mid levels of arousal but is poor at very low or very high levels.*

One way of raising arousal is to give rest breaks, though what you do during this time is important. Ideally it should be something which gives sensory variation; taking some exercise, for example, works well. Simply sitting in the car as a break from driving or watching another radar operator monitor a screen during your tea break does not provide the same variety. Loud noise also raises arousal. Wilkinson (1963) tested participants in conditions of sleep deprivation and in loud noise. Both showed reduced performance compared to their usual scores. When they had both sleep deprivation and loud noise together though, their performance was unaffected.

▶ How does Wilkinson's research support the inverted U arousal and performance curve?

▷ Performance is reduced in noise — this could be due to overarousal. It is also reduced in sleep deprivation — this could be due to underarousal. The unchanged performance when participants have both together could be because they cancel each other out so that arousal is in the middle of the curve, coinciding with the best performance.

To summarize, vigilance tasks are monotonous, boring and underarousing. Performance declines quite quickly and both sorts of errors are likely to occur — both false positives and false negatives. Performance can be improved by knowledge of results. This allows the worker to anticipate and raises motivation. Performance can also be improved by raising arousal. This can best be done by giving frequent rest breaks with a change of activity.

SAQ
7

A company is installing its first fish-locating sonar device in a new trawler. It needs to be watched continually and is presently in an isolated cabin. Shoals of fish are hard to discriminate from other small spots of 'noise' on the screen and the time to respond to a signal from a shoal is short. Advise the company how to get the best results from its new machine by helping its operators avoid, as far as possible, the difficulties with sustained attention that we have discussed above.

Checklist

1. Like research into selective attention, research into sustained attention or vigilance was prompted by practical, human problems.

2. Typically, vigilance task performance declines quite quickly during the first 30 minutes and more slowly thereafter.

3. Performance is improved if the operator has immediate knowledge of results and if arousal can be maintained at an optimal level.

ASSIGNMENTS

TUTOR ASSESSMENT

Please write one of the following essays to hand in to your tutor for marking. Once you have completed your reading and planning try to write the essay in a maximum of 45 minutes.

- ❏ How have psychologists sought to explain selective attention? To what extent have they been successful?

- ❏ Using evidence, show how it is possible to undertake two or more tasks simultaneously and discuss factors which limit this ability.

- ❏ What factors contribute to poor performance on a vigilance task? How can an operator be helped to improve performance?

- ❏ Critically evaluate the capacity model of attention.

- ❏ Using evidence, discuss the proposition that selecting material to attend to takes place before any semantic analysis of the material.

ESSAY PLANS

In addition to writing one essay, to assist your examination preparation make essay plans for a further *three* titles and give these to your tutor for marking and discussion.

FURTHER READING

RADFORD, J. and GOVIER, E. (Eds.) (1991) A *Textbook of Psychology*, 2nd edn. London: Routledge. [Few introductory texts devote more than a few pages to attention, but this one gives a short and up-to-date review at the end of a chapter on basic perceptual processes.]

SLACK, J. (1990) Attention. In Roth, I. *Introduction to Psychology, Vol. 2*. Hove: Lawrence Erlbaum and the Open University. [This two-volume text aimed at undergraduates studying psychology for the first time is very well laid-out, clear, detailed and accessible. Vol. 2 contains a 42-page chapter on attention by Jon Slack.]

GREENE, J. and HICKS, C. (1984) *Basic Cognitive Processes*. Milton Keynes: Open University Press. [This is in the open guides to psychology series and contains a 19-page module or chapter on attention. It is older and less detailed than the chapter by Slack, but has been designed as a revision text.]

EYSENCK, M.W. and KEENE, M.T. (1990) *Cognitive Psychology: A student's handbook*. Hove: Lawrence Erlbaum. [This is an up-to-date and comprehensive textbook. The 36-page chapter on attention and performance limitations is not difficult to read, but it is more demanding than the other suggestions I have listed This will take you further than this Unit and contains useful reading suggestions of its own, including references to primary sources.]

REFERENCES

Students studying psychology at pre-degree level, whether in schools, FE colleges or evening institutes, seldom have access to a well-stocked academic library; nor is it expected that they will have consulted all the original references. For most purposes, the books recommended in Further Reading will be adequate. This list is included for the use of those planning a full-scale project on this topic, and also for the sake of completeness.

ALLPORT, D.A. (1980) Attention and performance. In Claxton, G. (Ed.) *Cognitive Psychology: New directions*. London: Routledge & Kegan Paul.

ALLPORT, D.A., ANTONIS, B. and REYNOLDS, P. (1972) On the division of attention: a disproof of the single channel hypothesis. *Quarterly Journal of Experimental Psychology*, 24, 225-235.

BROADBENT, D. (1958) *Perception and Communication*. Oxford: Pergamon.

CASSELLS, A. (1991) *Remembering and Forgetting*. Leicester: BPS Books.

CHERRY, E.C. (1953) Some experiments on the recognition of speech, with one and two ears. *Journal of the Acoustical Society of America*, 25, 975-979.

CORTEEN, R.S. and WOOD, B. (1972) Autonomic responses to shock-associated words in an unattended channel. *Journal of Experimental Psychology*, 94, 308-313.

DAWSON, M.E. and SCHELL, A.M. (1982) Electrodermal responses to attended and unattended significant stimuli during dichotic listening. *Journal of Experimental Psychology: Human Perception and Performance*, 8, 82-86.

DEUTSCH, J.A. and DEUTSCH, D. (1963) Attention: some theoretical considerations, *Psychological Review*, 70, 80-90.

EYSENCK, M.W. and KEANE, M.T. (1990) *Cognitive Psychology: A student's handbook*. Hove: Lawrence Erlbaum.

FODOR, J. (1983) *Modularity of Mind*. Cambridge, MA: MIT Press.

GOVIER, E. and GOVIER, H. (1991) Basic perceptual processes. In Radford, J. and Govier, E. (Eds.) A *Textbook of Psychology* (2nd edn). London: Routledge.

GRAY, J.A. and WEDDERBURN, A.A.I. (1960) Grouping strategies with simultaneous stimuli. *Quarterly Journal of Experimental Psychology*, 12, 180-184.

JAMES, W. (1890) *The Principles of Psychology*, Vol. I. New York: Henry Holt.

KAHNEMAN, D. (1973) *Attention and Effort*. Englewood Cliffs, NJ: Prentice-Hall.

LOGAN, G.D. (1988) Toward an instance theory of automisation. *Psychological Review*, 95, 492-527.

McKAY, D.G. (1973) Aspects of the theory of comprehension, memory and attention. *Quarterly Journal of Experimental Psychology*, 25, 22-40.

MACKWORTH, N.H. (1950) Researches in the measurement of human performance. MRC *Special Report Series, no.* 268. H.M.S.O.

MORAY, N. (1969) *Attention: Selective processes in vision and hearing*. London: Hutchinson.

NEWSTEAD, S.E. and DENNIS, I. (1979) Lexical and grammatical processing of unshadowed messages: a re-examination of the McKay effect. *Quarterly Journal of Experimental Psychology*, 31, 477-488.

NORMAN, D.A. and SHALLICE, T. (1980) Attention to action: willed and automatic control of behaviour. CHIP *report* 99. San Diego, CA: University of California, San Diego.

REASON, J. (1987) The Chernobyl errors. *Bulletin of The British Psychological Society*, 40, 201-206.

SHAFFER, L.H. (1975) Multiple attention in continuous verbal tasks. In Rabbitt, P.M.A. and Dornic, S. (Eds.) *Attention and Performance*: V. London: Academic Press.

SHIFFRIN, R.M. and SCHNEIDER, W. (1977) Controlled and automatic human information processing: II Perceptual learning, automatic attending and a general theory. *Psychological Review*, 84, 127-190.

TREISMAN, A. (1960) Contextual cues in selective listening. *Quarterly Journal of Psychology*, 12, 242-248.

TREISMAN, A. (1964) Verbal cues, language and meaning in selective attention. *American Journal of Psychology*, 77, 206-219.

TREISMAN, A. and GELADE, G. (1980) A feature integration theory of attention. *Cognitive Psychology*, 12, 97-136.

WATSON, J.B. (1924) *Behaviourism*. Chicago: University of Chicago Press.

WEXLER, B.E. (1988) Dichotic presentation as a method for single hemisphere stimulation studies. In Hugdahl, K. (Ed.) *Handbook of Dichotic Listening: Theory, methods and research*. Chichester: Wiley.

WILKINSON, R.T. (1963) Interaction of noise with knowledge of results and sleep deprivation. *Journal of Experimental Psychology*, 66, 332-337.

GLOSSARY [Terms in bold type also appear as a separate entry]

Attention: it is difficult to define attention adequately, but it is usually defined as selecting one of several possible stimuli to concentrate conscious awareness on. The term has sometimes been used as an alternative to consciousness and it can also refer to automatic performance.

Attenuation: a process in which non-attended stimuli are not discarded entirely, but have their intensity reduced — usually to below **threshold** intensity. (An attenuator is the opposite of an amplifier.)

Automatic performance: refers to the way in which well-learned skills can be utilized without conscious attention. For example, an older child can work without conscious attention, a toddler cannot.

Behaviourism: the approach in psychology advocated by John B. Watson — that psychology should limit itself to observable, measurable phenomena which can be investigated with scientific rigour (i.e. behaviour and not internal mental events).

Capacity model: Kahneman's model of information processing in which processing capacity can be allocated flexibly within an overall capacity limit.

Central processor: this refers to Kahneman's capacity model in which processing capacity is not dedicated to any particular input, but can be allocated centrally and flexibly. (See *modular processing* for contrast.)

Channel: is a term borrowed from information theory. The individual can be seen as an information processing channel with receptors (eyes, ears) providing input, and behavioural responses representing output. A part of an individual could also be a channel, for example vision.

EEG (electroencephalogram): electrodes are attached to the scalp to detect changes in electrical potential in the brain. These can be transferred to paper as a continuous print-out. There are identifiable changes in electrical potential associated with different activities — for example different levels of sleep.

Dichotic listening: listening to two different messages at the same time with one message presented to each ear.

Enduring dispositions: personality factors, aspects of a person that are consistent in different circumstances.

False negative: missing a signal in a vigilance task for example; when searching for a signal incorrectly identifying it as absent.

False positive: the opposite of *false negative*. Identifying a signal as present when it is absent.

Filter model: a model concerned with how incoming stimuli are selected or rejected for further processing and attention.

Input: something put into a system. What you see or hear is input.

Introspection: looking inwards and observing your own conscious experiences.

Late selection model: a model of selective attention in which selection for conscious attention takes place after semantic analysis.

Modular processing: cognitive neuropsychologists assume that information processing is modular; that is, processing tasks are undertaken by numbers of independent processing modules dedicated to those particular tasks.

Parallel processing: refers to more than one information processing task being carried out simultaneously — for example chatting while riding a bicycle.

Selective attention: the focusing of attention on one stimulus to the exclusion of others.

Semantic processing or analysis: the analysis of the meaning of a message or stimulus.

Sensory modes: simply refers to our senses: taste, touch and so on.

Serial processing: information processing in which tasks are carried out in series or sequence. For example, you will not be able to listen to both inputs at once in a dichotic listening task. The only way to follow both is to switch rapidly back and forth between them — serial processing. Contrast with *parallel processing*.

Shadowing: repeating aloud immediately and fully a spoken message (presented in a dichotic listening task to one ear).

Short-term memory store: a limited capacity memory store able to hold 7 ± 2 chunks or items of information for only up to about 12 seconds, unless the items are rehearsed. Information in the short-term memory is in a relatively unprocessed form.

Sustained attention: a broad term referring to the continual searching for or attending to a stimulus.

Threshold: a boundary above which a stimulus will reach conscious attention and below which it will not.

Top-down processing: cognitive processing or analysis influenced by pre-existing assumptions about the data to be processed. (Bottom-up processing, on the other hand, is determined simply by the nature of the data — it is not influenced by past experience or assumptions about the data to be processed.)

Vigilance: see *sustained attention*.

ANSWERS TO SELF-ASSESSMENT QUESTIONS

SAQ 1 Example (i) could be told apart as the physical characteristics of the voices would differ quite a lot. The other two examples probably could not be.

SAQ 2 Broadbent's filter model proposes that non-attended stimuli are filtered out to allow us to selectively attend, to focus our conscious attention on a particular stimulus. He suggests that this filtering takes place without any reference to meaning (semantic content), only the physical characteristics of each stimulus are relevant.

Three pieces of evidence which suggest that this is not a complete model of selective attention are:

(1) Cherry's discovery that an unattended message can reach attention — the cocktail party phenomenon.

(2) Gray and Wedderburn's research showing that people did put two stimuli together so that they made sense.

(3) Research by Treisman using speech shadowing showing that material presented to the unattended ear could break through to attention under certain circumstances.

SAQ 3 (a) Treisman's model differs from Broadbent's by incorporating a second filter which allows items from unattended channels to reach attention under certain circumstances. Such items will have a reduced threshold because they have personal or contextual relevance.

(b) You would be more likely to hear the name Mozart because it is relevant to a conversation about classical music. The name Smith is unlikely to be.

(c) Your name, for example.

(d) Your name has a reduced threshold because of its personal relevance so that it intrudes into attention even from an unattended source.

SAQ 4 (a) The material reaches attention after semantic analysis which identifies it as relevant.

(b) Relevant material reaches attention because it has a reduced threshold.

(c) Broadbent's model does not account for these findings.

SAQ 5 (a) Processing of one item after another in series. Items requiring conscious attention can only be processed in series.

(b) Processing of two or more items at the same time. This can be done when a task is automatic.

SAQ 6 Treisman's model suggests that we hear our own name because it has a reduced threshold because of its personal relevance. Broadbent's model cannot explain this, Deutsch and Deutsch's model suggests that all material is analysed for meaning which seems implausible on the grounds of economy. Kahneman's model suggests that processing capacity would be allocated so that you would hear your name at a party because the capacity allocation policy would direct attention to items of personal or contextual importance or relevance. Neither Treisman's or Kahneman's account really explains wholly convincingly the mechanisms by which attention is directed. Both accounts are plausible. There is an interesting debate between them which is beyond our scope here. I prefer Treisman's approach as Kahneman's seems to imply another person inside our head making decisions!

SAQ 7 Crew need to have short periods watching the screen with a completely different task at other times. Perhaps two crew members on each six-hour watch could alternate the vigilance task every 30 minutes with a more physical and interactive task. Ideally, full feedback of performance should be given but this will not be possible on a trawler. As much feedback as possible should be given. An incentive bonus scheme could operate so that each positively identified contact is rewarded. A large number of crew members should be trained to use the machine. Knowledge of machine performance and of the behaviour of different species of shoals of fish under various conditions will help the operator to know what to expect.